Fair Isle
to CROCHET

MW01614558

Crocheting friends, Fair Isle isn't just for knitters!

When you make these five afghans, you'll easily get the same richly detailed look as knitted Fair Isle designs. It's as simple as using single crochet stitches and following our full-color stitch charts! The Southwest Warmth pattern offers muted sunset colors and is a perfect gift for a man. The Girl's Cozy Afghan is a vivid palette that includes purple and pink. The boys in the house will enjoy the Kid's Winter Warmer in orange, yellow, blue, and green. For babies, there is a soft flurry of snowflakes or a shower of sweet hearts. Even the finishing is a breeze on these designs, because the fringe doesn't require cutting extra yarn lengths. You just leave long ends at the sides of the afghan; then tie them together. Have fun creating your family's very own Fair Isle afghans—in crochet!

LEISURE ARTS, INC.
Little Rock, Arkansas

Southwest Warmth

◼◼◼◻ INTERMEDIATE

Finished Size: 46³/₄" w x 68¹/₂" l, excluding fringe (119 cm x 174 cm)

MATERIALS

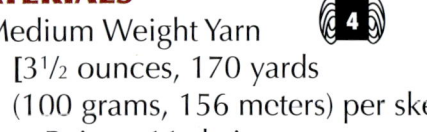

Medium Weight Yarn
[3¹/₂ ounces, 170 yards
(100 grams, 156 meters) per skein]:
Beige - 11 skeins
Gold - 3 skeins
Dark Red - 3 skeins
Burnt Orange - 3 skeins
Crochet hook, size I (5.5 mm) **or** size needed for
gauge
Yarn needle

GAUGE: In pattern, 16 sc and 12 rows = 4" (10 cm)

Gauge Swatch: 4" (10 cm) square
Ch 16; finish off.
Row 1 (Right side): Working in back ridge only of
ch **(Fig. 1, page 19)**, join yarn with sc in first ch **(see
Joining With Sc, page 19)**; sc in each ch across;
finish off.
Rows 2-12: With **right** side facing and working in
Back Loops Only **(Fig. 2, page 19)**, join yarn with sc
in first sc; sc in each sc across; finish off.

Always join yarn and finish off leaving an 8"
(20.5 cm) end for fringe. When working rows
with two colors, leave an 8" (20.5 cm) end
of second color at beginning, and work each
st with the first color over the second color
across to first st of second color. At end of
row, work over second color to end; finish off
working yarn and cut second color leaving 8"
(20.5 cm) ends.

Every row is a **right** side row and is worked in
Back Loops Only **(Fig. 2, page 19)**.

When changing color **(Fig. 3, page 19)**, work
over color not being used, holding it with
normal tension.

Instructions begin on page 4.

With Beige and leaving an 8" (20.5 cm) end at beginning, ch 187; finish off leaving an 8" (20.5 cm) end.

Row 1 (Right side)**:** Working in back ridge only of ch *(Fig. 1, page 19)*, join Beige with sc in first ch *(see Joining with Sc, page 19)*; sc in each ch across; finish off: 187 sc.

Note: Loop a short piece of yarn around any stitch to mark Row 1 as **right** side.

Row 2: With **right** side facing and working in Back Loops Only *(Fig. 2, page 19)*, join Beige with sc in first sc, sc in each sc across; finish off.

Row 3: Begin following Chart as follows: with **right** side facing, working in Back Loops Only, leaving an 8" (20.5 cm) end of each color, and working over Gold, join Beige with sc in first sc; sc in next 2 sc, with Gold, sc in next sc, ★ with Beige, sc in next 5 sc, with Gold, sc in next 4 sc, with Beige, sc in next 5 sc, with Gold, sc in next sc; repeat from ★ across to last 3 sc, with Beige and working over Gold, sc in last 3 sc; finish off Beige and cut Gold.

Rows 4-38: Continue following Chart, working marked stitch repeat 6 times across each row before working last st, beginning with Row 4 and working through Row 38.

Rows 39-205: Repeat Chart Rows 1-38, 4 times; then repeat Chart Rows 1-15 once **more**.

FINISHING
Tie groups of 6 ends together in an overhand knot to form fringe along side edges of afghan. Lay on a flat surface and trim to desired length.

CHART

Work pattern between arrows 6 times before working last st.

COLOR KEY:

☐ = BEIGE

☐ = GOLD

■ = DARK RED

■ = BURNT ORANGE

Girl's Cozy Afghan

INTERMEDIATE

Finished Size: 40½" w x 49" l, excluding fringe (103 cm x 124.5 cm)

MATERIALS

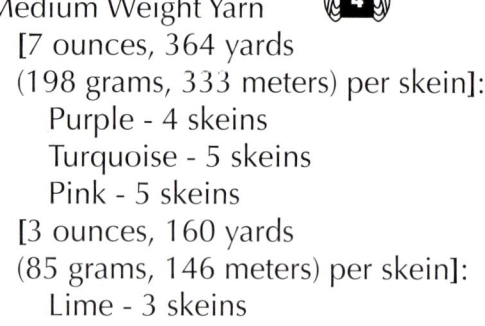

Medium Weight Yarn

[7 ounces, 364 yards
(198 grams, 333 meters) per skein]:

    Purple - 4 skeins
    Turquoise - 5 skeins
    Pink - 5 skeins

[3 ounces, 160 yards
(85 grams, 146 meters) per skein]:

    Lime - 3 skeins

Crochet hook, size I (5.5 mm) **or** size
    needed for gauge

Yarn needle

GAUGE: In pattern, 12 sc and 10 rows = 4" (10 cm)

Gauge Swatch: 4" (10 cm) square
Ch 12; finish off.
Row 1 (Right side)**:** Working in back ridge only of ch **(Fig. 1, page 19)**, join yarn with sc in first ch **(see Joining With Sc, page 19)**; sc in each ch across; finish off.
Rows 2-10: With **right** side facing and working in Back Loops Only **(Fig. 2, page 19)**, join yarn with sc in first sc; sc in each sc across; finish off.

Always join yarn and finish off leaving an 8" (20.5 cm) end for fringe. When working rows with two colors, leave an 8" (20.5 cm) end of second color at beginning, and work each st with the first color over the second color across to first st of second color. At end of row, work over second color to end; finish off working yarn and cut second color leaving 8" (20.5 cm) ends.

Every row is a **right** side row and is worked in Back Loops Only **(Fig. 2, page 19)**.

When changing color **(Fig. 3, page 19)**, work over color not being used, holding it with normal tension.

Instructions begin on page 8.

With Purple and leaving an 8" (20.5 cm) end at beginning, ch 122; finish off leaving an 8" (20.5 cm) end.

Row 1 (Right side)**:** Working in back ridge only of ch *(Fig. 1, page 19)*, join Purple with sc in first ch *(see Joining with Sc, page 19)*; sc in each ch across; finish off: 122 sc.

Note: Loop a short piece of yarn around any stitch to mark Row 1 as **right** side.

Row 2: With **right** side facing and working in Back Loops Only *(Fig. 2, page 19)*, join Purple with sc in first sc; sc in each sc across; finish off.

Row 3: Begin following Chart as follows: with **right** side facing, working in Back Loops Only, leaving an 8" (20.5 cm) end of each color, and working over Lime, join Purple with sc in first sc; with Lime, sc in next sc, ★ with Purple, sc in next 3 sc, with Lime, sc in next sc; repeat from ★ across to last 4 sc, with Purple and working over Lime, sc in last 4 sc; finish off Purple and cut Lime.

Rows 4-36: Continue following Chart, working marked stitch repeat 5 times across each row before working last st, beginning with Row 4 and working through Row 36.

Rows 37-121: Repeat Chart Rows 3-36 twice, then repeat Chart Rows 3-19 once **more**.

Rows 122 and 123: With **right** side facing, join Purple with sc in first sc, sc in each sc across; finish off.

FINISHING
Tie groups of 6 ends together in an overhand knot to form fringe along side edges of afghan. Lay on a flat surface and trim to desired length.

COLOR KEY:

■ = PURPLE

■ = LIME

■ = TURQUOISE

■ = PINK

CHART

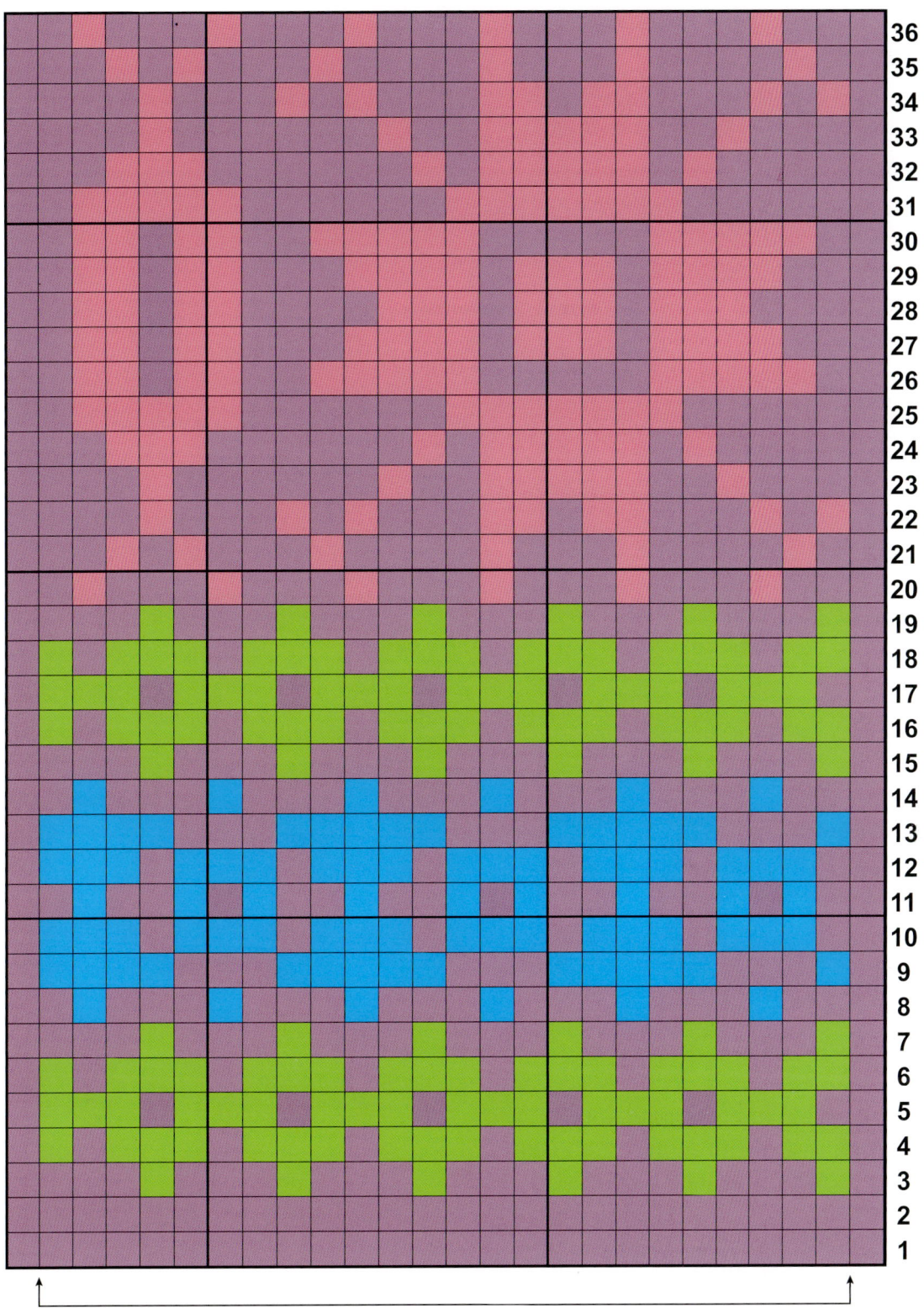

Work pattern between arrows 5 times before working last st.

Kid's Winter Warmer

⬛⬛⬛⬜ **INTERMEDIATE**

Shown on page 1

Finished Size: 40" w x 46" l, excluding fringe (101.5 cm x 117 cm)

MATERIALS

MEDIUM 4

Medium Weight Yarn
   [6 ounces, 315 yards
   (170 grams, 287 meters) per skein]:
      Orange - 2 skeins
      Yellow - 1 skein
      Lime Green - 2 skeins
      Turquoise - 1 skein
Crochet hook, size J (6 mm) **or** size needed for
   gauge
Yarn needle

GAUGE: In pattern, 12 sc and 10 rows = 4" (10 cm)

Gauge Swatch: 4" (10 cm) square
Ch 12; finish off.
Row 1 (Right side)**:** Working in back ridge only of
ch *(Fig. 1, page 19)*, join yarn with sc in first ch *(see
Joining With Sc, page 19)*; sc in each ch across;
finish off.
Rows 2-10: With **right** side facing and working in
Back Loops Only *(Fig. 2, page 19)*, join yarn with sc
in first sc; sc in each sc across; finish off.

Always join yarn and finish off leaving an 8"
(20.5 cm) end for fringe. When working rows
with two colors, leave an 8" (20.5 cm) end
of second color at beginning, and work each
st with the first color over the second color
across to first st of second color. At end of
row, work over second color to end; finish off
working yarn and cut second color leaving 8"
(20.5 cm) ends.

Every row is a **right** side row and is worked in
Back Loops Only *(Fig. 2, page 19)*.

When changing color *(Fig. 3, page 19)*, work
over color not being used, holding it with
normal tension.

With Orange and leaving an 8" (20.5 cm) end at beginning, ch 120; finish off leaving an 8" (20.5 cm) end.

Row 1 (Right side): Working in back ridge only of ch *(Fig. 1, page 19)*, join Orange with sc in first ch *(see Joining with Sc, page 19)*; sc in each ch across; finish off: 120 sc.

Note: Loop a short piece of yarn around any stitch to mark Row 1 as **right** side.

Row 2: Begin following Chart as follows: with **right** side facing, working in Back Loops Only *(Fig. 2, page 19)*, leaving an 8" (20.5 cm) end of each color, and working over Yellow, join Orange with sc in first sc; with Yellow, sc in next 2 sc, ★ with Orange, sc in next 2 sc, with Yellow, sc in next 2 sc; repeat from ★ across to last st, with Orange and working over Yellow, sc in last sc; finish off Orange and cut Yellow.

Rows 3-36: Continue following Chart, working marked stitch repeat 6 times across each row, beginning with Row 3 and working through Row 36.

Rows 37-115: Repeat Chart Rows 1-36 twice, then repeat Chart Rows 1-7 once **more**.

FINISHING
Tie groups of 6 ends together in an overhand knot to form fringe along side edges of afghan. Lay on a flat surface and trim to desired length.

CHART

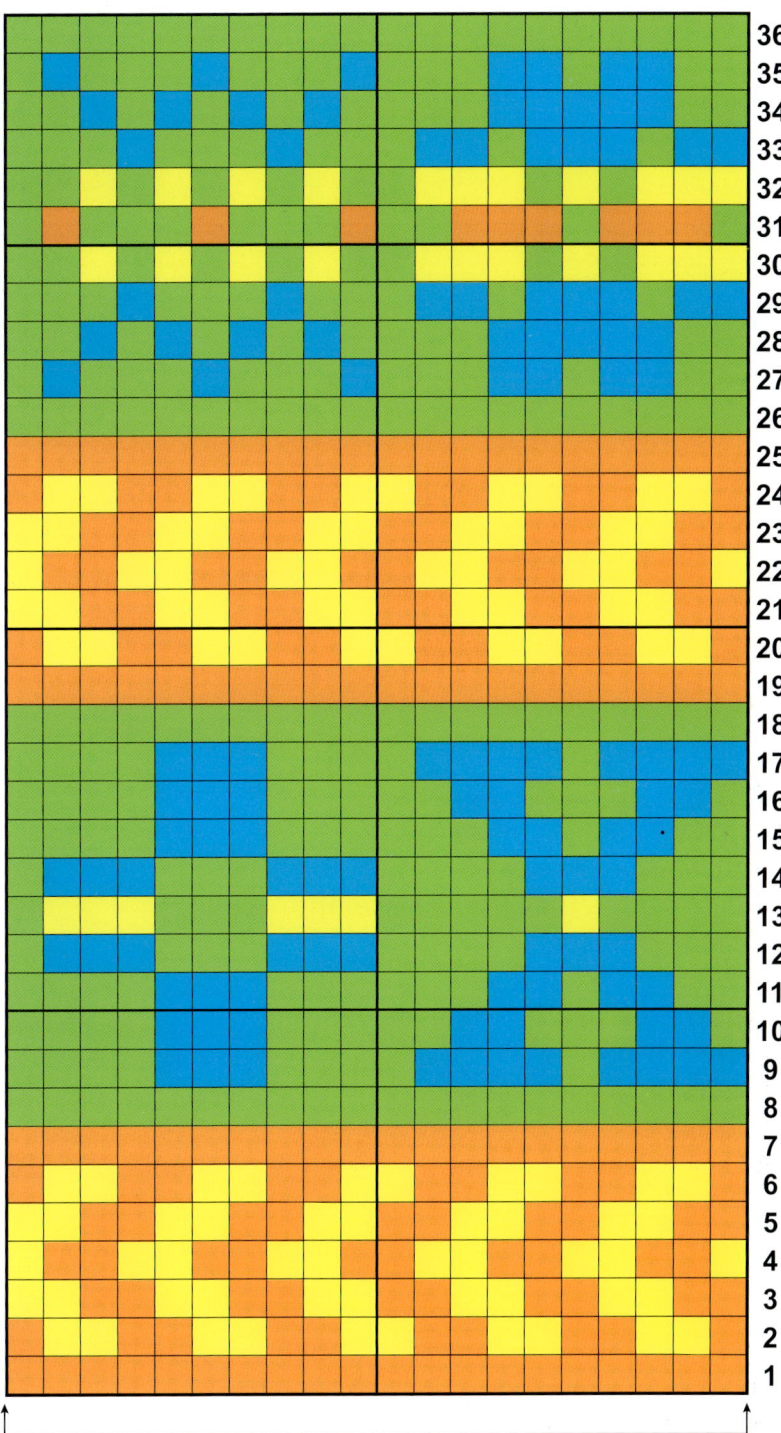

Work pattern between arrows 6 times.

COLOR KEY:

◼ = ORANGE

◻ = YELLOW

◼ = LIME GREEN

◼ = TURQUOISE

Baby Snowflakes

◼◼◼◻ INTERMEDIATE

Finished Size: 37³/₄" w x 38¹/₄" l, excluding fringe (96 cm x 97 cm)

MATERIALS

LIGHT 3

Light Weight Yarn
[5 ounces, 459 yards
(141 grams, 420 meters) per skein]:
    Blue - 2 skeins
    White - 2 skeins
Crochet hook, size G (4 mm) **or** size needed for
  gauge
Yarn needle

GAUGE: In pattern, 16 sc and 14 rows = 4" (10 cm)

Gauge Swatch: 4" (10 cm) square
Ch 16; finish off.
Row 1 (Right side)**:** Working in back ridge only of
ch **(Fig. 1, page 19)**, join yarn with sc in first ch **(see
Joining With Sc, page 19)**; sc in each ch across;
finish off.
Rows 2-14: With **right** side facing and working in
Back Loops Only **(Fig. 2, page 19)**, join yarn with sc
in first sc; sc in each sc across; finish off.

Always join yarn and finish off leaving an 8"
(20.5 cm) end for fringe. When working rows
with two colors, leave an 8" (20.5 cm) end
of second color at beginning, and work each
st with the first color over the second color
across to first st of second color. At end of
row, work over second color to end; finish off
working yarn and cut second color leaving 8"
(20.5 cm) ends.

Every row is a **right** side row and is worked in
Back Loops Only **(Fig. 2, page 19)**.

When changing color **(Fig. 3, page 19)**, work
over color not being used, holding it with
normal tension.

Instructions begin on page 14.

With Blue and leaving an 8" (20.5 cm) end at beginning, ch 151; finish off leaving an 8" (20.5 cm) end.

Row 1 (Right side)**:** Working in back ridge only of ch **(Fig. 1, page 19)**, join Blue with sc in first ch **(see Joining with Sc, page 19)**; sc in each ch across; finish off: 151 sc.

Note: Loop a short piece of yarn around any stitch to mark Row 1 as **right** side.

Rows 2 and 3: With **right** side facing and working in Back Loops Only **(Fig. 2, page 19)**, join Blue with sc in first sc; sc in each sc across; finish off.

Row 4: Begin following Chart as follows: with **right** side facing, leaving an 8" (20.5 cm) end of each color, and working over White, join Blue with sc in first sc; ★ with White, sc in next 2 sc, with Blue, sc in next sc; repeat from ★ across; finish off Blue and cut White.

Rows 5-35: Continue following Chart, working marked stitch repeat 6 times across each row, beginning with Row 5 and working through Row 35.

Rows 36-131: Repeat Chart Rows 4-35, 3 times.

Rows 132-134: Repeat Chart Rows 1-3.

FINISHING

Tie groups of 6 ends together in an overhand knot to form fringe along side edges of afghan. Lay on a flat surface and trim to desired length.

COLOR KEY:

☐ = BLUE

☐ = WHITE

CHART

Work pattern between arrows 6 times.

Baby Hearts

◀■■■▭ INTERMEDIATE

Shown on back cover

Finished Size: 36¹/₂" w x 42¹/₂" l, excluding fringe (93 cm x 108 cm)

MATERIALS

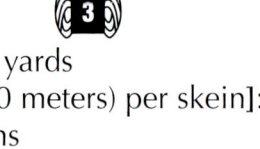

Light Weight Yarn
   [5 ounces, 459 yards
   (141 grams, 420 meters) per skein]:
      Pink - 3 skeins
      White - 2 skeins
Crochet hook, size G (4 mm) **or** size needed for
   gauge
Yarn needle

GAUGE: In pattern, 16 sc and 14 rows = 4" (10 cm)

Gauge Swatch: 4" (10 cm) square
Ch 16; finish off.
Row 1 (Right side)**:** Working in back ridge only of
ch *(Fig. 1, page 19)*, join yarn with sc in first ch *(see
Joining With Sc, page 19)*; sc in each ch across;
finish off.
Rows 2-14: With **right** side facing and working in
Back Loops Only *(Fig. 2, page 19)*, join yarn with sc
in first sc; sc in each sc across; finish off.

Always join yarn and finish off leaving an 8"
(20.5 cm) end for fringe. When working rows
with two colors, leave an 8" (20.5 cm) end
of second color at beginning, and work each
st with the first color over the second color
across to first st of second color. At end of
row, work over second color to end; finish off
working yarn and cut second color leaving 8"
(20.5 cm) ends.

Every row is a **right** side row and is worked in
Back Loops Only *(Fig. 2, page 19)*.

When changing color *(Fig. 3, page 19)*, work
over color not being used, holding it with
normal tension.

With Pink and leaving an 8"
(20.5 cm) end at beginning, ch 146;
finish off leaving an 8" (20.5 cm) end.

Row 1 (Right side)**:** Working in back
ridge only of ch *(Fig. 1, page 19)*, join
Pink with sc in first ch *(see Joining
with Sc, page 19)*; sc in each ch across;
finish off: 146 sc.

Note: Loop a short piece of yarn
around any stitch to mark Row 1 as
right side.

Rows 2 and 3: With **right** side facing
and working in Back Loops Only *(Fig.
2, page 19)*, join Pink with sc in first sc,
sc in each sc across; finish off.

Row 4: Begin following Chart as
follows: with **right** side facing, leaving
an 8" (20.5 cm) end of each color, and
working over White, join Pink with sc
in first sc; sc in next 2 sc, with White,
sc in next 3 sc, ★ with Pink, sc in next
3 sc, with White, sc in next 3 sc; repeat
from ★ across to last 2 sc, with Pink
and working over White, sc in last 2 sc;
finish off Pink and cut White.

Rows 5-42: Continue following Chart,
working marked stitch repeat 6 times
across each row before working last st,
beginning with
Row 5 and working through Row 42.

Rows 43-146: Repeat Chart Rows 2-42
twice, then repeat Chart Rows 2-23
once **more**.

Rows 147-149: Repeat Chart Rows 1-3.

FINISHING
Tie groups of 6 ends together in an
overhand knot to form fringe along side
edges of afghan. Lay on a flat surface
and trim to desired length.

CHART

Work pattern between arrows 6 times before working last st.

COLOR KEY:

■ = PINK

□ = WHITE

General Instructions

ABBREVIATIONS

cm	centimeters
ch(s)	chain(s)
mm	millimeter(s)
sc	single crochet(s)
st(s)	stitch(es)
YO	yarn over

★ — work instructions following ★ as many **more** times as indicated in addition to the first time.

( ) — contains explanatory remarks.

colon (:) — the number given after a colon at the end of a row denotes the number of stitches you should have on that row.

GAUGE

Exact gauge is **essential** for proper size. Before beginning your project, make the sample swatch given in the individual instructions in the yarn and hook specified. After completing the swatch, measure it, counting your stitches and rows carefully. If your swatch is larger or smaller than specified, **make another, changing hook size to get the correct gauge**. Keep trying until you find the size hook that will give you the specified gauge. Once proper gauge is obtained, measure width of afghan approximately every 3" (7.5 cm) to be sure gauge remains consistent.

Yarn Weight Symbol & Names	LACE 0	SUPER FINE 1	FINE 2	LIGHT 3	MEDIUM 4	BULKY 5	SUPER BULKY 6
Type of Yarns in Category	Fingering, 10-count crochet thread	Sock, Fingering Baby	Sport, Baby	DK, Light Worsted	Worsted, Afghan, Aran	Chunky, Craft, Rug	Bulky, Roving
Crochet Gauge* Ranges in Single Crochet to 4" (10 cm)	32-42 double crochets**	21-32 sts	16-20 sts	12-17 sts	11-14 sts	8-11 sts	5-9 sts
Advised Hook Size Range	Steel*** 6,7,8 Regular hook B-1	B-1 to E-4	E-4 to 7	7 to I-9	I-9 to K-10.5	K-10.5 to M-13	M-13 and larger

*GUIDELINES ONLY: The chart above reflects the most commonly used gauges and hook sizes for specific yarn categories.

** Lace weight yarns are usually crocheted on larger-size hooks to create lacy openwork patterns. Accordingly, a gauge range is difficult to determine. Always follow the gauge stated in your pattern.

*** Steel crochet hooks are sized differently from regular hooks–the higher the number the smaller the hook, which is the reverse of regular hook sizing.

CROCHET TERMINOLOGY	
UNITED STATES	INTERNATIONAL
slip stitch (slip st) =	single crochet (sc)
single crochet (sc) =	double crochet (dc)
half double crochet (hdc) =	half treble crochet (htr)
double crochet (dc) =	treble crochet(tr)
treble crochet (tr) =	double treble crochet (dtr)
double treble crochet (dtr) =	triple treble crochet (ttr)
triple treble crochet (tr tr) =	quadruple treble crochet (qtr)
skip =	miss

◼◻◻◻ BEGINNER	Projects for first-time crocheters using basic stitches. Minimal shaping.
◼◼◻◻ EASY	Projects using yarn with basic stitches, repetitive stitch patterns, simple color changes, and simple shaping and finishing.
◼◼◼◻ INTERMEDIATE	Projects using a variety of techniques, such as basic lace patterns or color patterns, mid-level shaping and finishing.
◼◼◼◼ EXPERIENCED	Projects with intricate stitch patterns, techniques and dimension, such as non-repeating patterns, multi-color techniques, fine threads, small hooks, detailed shaping and refined finishing.

CROCHET HOOKS												
U.S.	B-1	C-2	D-3	E-4	F-5	G-6	H-8	I-9	J-10	K-10½	N	P	Q
Metric - mm	2.25	2.75	3.25	3.5	3.75	4	5	5.5	6	6.5	9	10	15

JOINING WITH SC

When instructed to join with sc, begin with a slip knot on hook. Insert hook in stitch or space indicated, YO and pull up a loop, YO and draw through both loops on hook.

BACK RIDGE

Work only in loops indicated by arrows *(Fig. 1)*.

Fig. 1

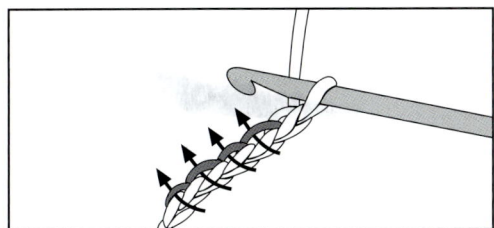

BACK LOOP ONLY

Work only in loop indicated by arrow *(Fig. 2)*.

Fig. 2

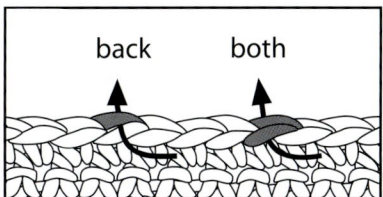

CHANGING COLORS

Insert hook in stitch indicated, YO and pull up a loop, drop yarn, with new yarn *(Fig. 3)*, YO and draw through both loops on hook.

Fig. 3

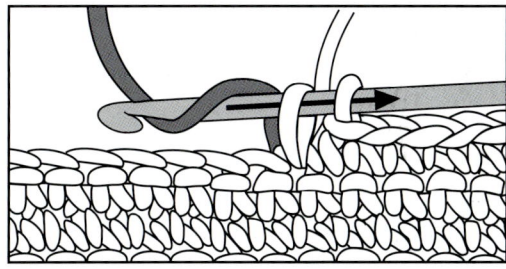

Production Team: Technical Editor - Joan Beebe; Graphic Artist - Liz Field; Photo Stylist - Sondra Daniel; and Photographer - Ken West.

For digital downloads of Leisure Arts' best-selling designs, visit http://www.leisureartslibrary.com

Instructions tested and photo models made by Marianna Crowder, Freda Gillham, and Raymelle Greening.

We have made every effort to ensure that these instructions are accurate and complete. We cannot, however, be responsible for human error, typographical mistakes, or variations in individual work.

YARN INFORMATION

The afghans in this leaflet were made using various weights of yarn. Any brand of the specified weight of yarn may be used. It is best to refer to the yardage/meters when determining how many balls or skeins to purchase. Remember, to arrive at the finished size, it is the GAUGE/TENSION that is important, not the brand of yarn. For your convenience, listed below are the specific yarns used to create our photography models.

SOUTHWEST WARMTH
Lion Brand® Vanna's Choice®
Beige - #123 Beige
Gold - #130 Honey
Dark Red - #133 Brick
Burnt Orange - #135 Rust

GIRL'S COZY AFGHAN
Red Heart® Super Saver®
Purple - #528 Medium Purple
Turquoise - #512 Turqua
Pink - #722 Pretty 'n Pink
Lime - #655 Lime

KID'S WINTER WARMER
Caron® Simply Soft® Brites
Orange - #9605 Mango
Yellow - #9606 Lemonade
Lime Green - #9607 Limelight
Turquoise - #9608 Blue Mint

BABY SNOWFLAKES
Lion Brand® Babysoft®
Blue - #106 Pastel Blue
White - #100 White

BABY HEARTS
Lion Brand® Babysoft®
Pink - #141 Pink Lemonade
White - #100 White